To:

From:

Date:

Coloring FAITH

Morning has Broken

An Inspirational
Coloring Book
Celebrating God's Creation

Illustrated by
Jennifer Tucker

ZONDERVAN®

ZONDERVAN

Morning Has Broken

Copyright © Zondervan 2023

Illustrations © 2023 Jennifer Tucker

Visit www.zondervan.com.

Requests for information should be addressed to: Zondervan, Grand Rapids, Michigan 49546

Art direction and cover: Sabryna Lugge
Interior illustrator: Jennifer Tucker
Interior design: Phoebe Wetherbee

ISBN: 978-0-3104-6317-7

Printed in India
23 24 25 26 27 REP 6 5 4 3 2 1

INTRODUCTION

Then God said, "I give you every seed-bearing plant on the face of the whole earth and every tree that has fruit with seed in it. They will be yours for food. And to all the beasts of the earth and all the birds in the sky and all the creatures that move along the ground—everything that has the breath of life in it—I give every green plant for food."

GENESIS 1:29–30

From the beginning, God has celebrated the bounty of the earth: the land, sea, seasons, animals, plants, and trees. He looked at His creation and saw that it was good. Then He gave all that to us to help us find peace, to find beauty, to find Him.

World events have made it more important than ever to make time to quiet our minds, connect with God, and immerse ourselves in the elements of nature He provided for us. The break of each morning is another opportunity for that connection.

Because our brains often jump from topic to topic, task to task, and crisis to crisis, many of us find it difficult to slow down and soak in God's goodness. We've created this beautiful coloring book to help you see the breaking of each morning in a new light—to breathe in and prepare for the craziness of life. There is nothing like the uplifting, stress-reducing activities of coloring and meditating on God's Word to help sharpen our focus.

Did you know that coloring can actually relax your brain? Like prayer or meditation, coloring reduces anxious thoughts, and when Bible verses and inspiring quotes are added, stress levels decrease and gratitude levels increase.

We hope you'll read the words in this book and feel motivated to pray or meditate on them while you color. More than anything, we hope this book will offer you calm moments to form a closer connection with God while you create art to keep. The perforated pages make it easy to tear out pieces of inspiration to frame or share with others. Some sections of the coloring pages are embellished with metallic ink to add an extra glimmer to your completed pieces of art. We suggest you not color over these areas but let them complement your coloring choices or inspire you to try metallic pens!

Want to share your artwork and inspiring words with even more people? Post your images on social media and use the hashtag #coloringfaith. Also, find more gorgeous coloring books at Coloringfaith.com.

God called the light "day," and the darkness he called "night."
And there was evening, and there was morning—the first day.

GENESIS 1:5

Wild roses are fairest, and nature a better gardener than art.

LOUISA MAY ALCOTT

Wild roses are fairest, and nature a better gardener than art.

LOUISA MAY ALCOTT

He has made everything beautiful in its time.

ECCLESIASTES 3:11

HE MADE YOU
SO YOU COULD SHARE IN HIS CREATION,
COULD LOVE & LAUGH & KNOW HIM.

Ted Griffin

He made you so you could share in His creation,
could love and laugh and know Him.

TED GRIFFIN

THE WHOLE EARTH IS FILLED WITH AWE AT YOUR WONDERS;
WHERE MORNING DAWNS, WHERE EVENING FADES,
YOU CALL FORTH SONGS OF JOY.

PSALM 65:8

The whole earth is filled with awe at your wonders;
where morning dawns, where evening fades,
you call forth songs of joy.

PSALM 65:8

The whole world is a love letter from God.

PETER KREEFT

Flowers appear on the earth;
the Season of Singing has Come,
the cooing of doves is heard in our land.

SONG OF
SOLOMON
2:12

Flowers appear on the earth;
the season of singing has come,
the cooing of doves
is heard in our land.

SONG OF SOLOMON 2:12

Bright
were the blossoms
on every bough:

I trusted Him when
the roses were blooming;

*I trust **Him** now.*

L. B. COWMAN

Bright were the blossoms on every bough: I trusted Him
when the roses were blooming; I trust Him now.

L. B. COWMAN

Weeping may endure for a night,
but joy comes in the morning.

PSALM 30:5 NKJV

HOPE

BEGINS IN THE DARK,
THE STUBBORN HOPE THAT IF YOU JUST
SHOW UP AND TRY TO DO THE RIGHT THING,
THE DAWN WILL COME.

ANNE LAMOTT

Hope begins in the dark, the stubborn hope that if you just
show up and try to do the right thing, the dawn will come.

ANNE LAMOTT

You will go out in joy
and be led forth in peace;
the mountains and hills
will burst into song before you,
and all the trees of the field
will clap their hands.

ISAIAH 55:12

You will go out in joy
and be led forth in peace;
the mountains and hills
will burst into song before you,
and all the trees of the field
will clap their hands.

ISAIAH 55:12

THE CREATOR THINKS
ENOUGH OF YOU TO
HAVE SENT SOMEONE
VERY SPECIAL SO THAT
YOU MIGHT HAVE LIFE —
ABUNDANTLY,
JOYFULLY,
COMPLETELY,
AND VICTORIOUSLY.

Anonymous

The Creator thinks enough of you to have sent
Someone very special so that you might have life—
abundantly, joyfully, completely, and victoriously.

ANONYMOUS

Consider the lilies of the field

MATTHEW 6:28
NKJV

"Consider the lilies of the field, how they grow."

MATTHEW 6:28 NKJV

Where flowers bloom, so does hope.

LADY BIRD JOHNSON

Where flowers bloom, so does hope.

LADY BIRD JOHNSON

By wisdom
THE LORD LAID
THE EARTH'S FOUNDATIONS.

Proverbs 3:19

By wisdom the Lord laid the earth's foundations,
by understanding he set the heavens in place;
by his knowledge the watery depths were divided,
and the clouds let drop the dew.

PROVERBS 3:19–20

Some days,
it is enough encouragement
just to watch the clouds
break up and disappear,
leaving behind a blue patch of sky
and bright sunshine that is
so warm upon my face.

ANONYMOUS

Some days, it is enough encouragement just to watch the clouds break up and disappear, leaving behind a blue patch of sky and bright sunshine that is so warm upon my face. It's a glimpse of divinity; a kiss from heaven.

ANONYMOUS

Let the heavens rejoice,
let the earth be glad;
let the sea resound,
and all that is in it.

PSALM 96:11

Let the heavens rejoice, let the earth be glad;
let the sea resound, and all that is in it.

PSALM 96:11

I must have flowers, always, and always.

CLAUDE MONET

I must have flowers, always, and always.

CLAUDE MONET

Because of the LORD's great love we are not consumed,
for his compassions never fail.
They are new every morning;
great is your faithfulness.

LAMENTATIONS 3:22-23

GREAT OAKS FROM LITTLE ACORNS GROW

14th CENTURY PROVERB

Great oaks from little acorns grow.

14TH CENTURY PROVERB

In the morning, Lord, you hear my voice.

PSALM 5:3

In the morning, Lord, you hear my voice;
in the morning I lay my requests before you
and wait expectantly.

PSALM 5:3

I found the poems in the fields, And only wrote them down.

JOHN CLARE

I found the poems in the fields,
And only wrote them down.

JOHN CLARE

THE PATH OF THE RIGHTEOUS
IS LIKE THE MORNING SUN,
SHINING EVER BRIGHTER
TILL THE FULL LIGHT OF DAY.

PROVERBS 4:18

The path of the righteous is like the morning sun,
shining ever brighter till the full light of day.

PROVERBS 4:18

EVERYBODY NEEDS
BEAUTY AS WELL AS BREAD,
PLACES TO PLAY IN & PRAY IN,
WHERE NATURE MAY HEAL &
CHEER & AND GIVE STRENGTH
TO BODY AND SOUL ALIKE.

John Muir

Everybody needs beauty as well as bread, places to play in and pray in,
where Nature may heal and cheer and give strength to body and soul alike.

JOHN MUIR

"Consider THE Ravens:

THEY DO NOT SOW
OR REAP, THEY HAVE
NO STOREROOM OR BARN;
YET GOD FEEDS THEM.
AND HOW MUCH MORE
VALUABLE YOU ARE
THAN BIRDS!"

LUKE 12:24

"Consider the ravens: They do not sow or reap, they
have no storeroom or barn; yet God feeds them. And
how much more valuable you are than birds!"

LUKE 12:24

EVERYTHING BEAUTIFUL HAS A MARK OF ETERNITY.

SIMONE WEIL

Everything beautiful has a mark of eternity.

SIMONE WEIL

THROUGH HIM
ALL THINGS WERE MADE;
WITHOUT HIM
NOTHING WAS MADE
THAT HAS BEEN MADE.

John 1:3

Through him all things were made; without him
nothing was made that has been made.

JOHN 1:3

A light wind swept over the corn, and all nature laughed in the sunshine.

ANNE BRONTË

A light wind swept over the corn, and all
nature laughed in the sunshine.

ANNE BRONTË

The grass withers and the flowers fall, but the word of our God endures forever.

ISAIAH 40:8

The grass withers and the flowers fall,
but the word of our God endures forever.

ISAIAH 40:8

In all things of nature there is something of the marvelous.

ARISTOTLE

In all things of nature there is something of the marvelous.

ARISTOTLE

I PRAISE YOU
BECAUSE I AM
fearfully
AND
wonderfully
made;
YOUR WORKS ARE
WONDERFUL,
I KNOW THAT FULL WELL.

PSALM 139:14

I praise you because I am fearfully and wonderfully made;
your works are wonderful, I know that full well.

PSALM 139:14

Every green tree is far more glorious than if it were made of gold and silver.

MARTIN LUTHER

Every green tree is far more glorious than
if it were made of gold and silver.

MARTIN LUTHER

Awake, NORTH WIND, & come, SOUTH WIND! Blow on my garden, THAT ITS fragrance MAY SPREAD everywhere.

SONG OF SOLOMON 4:16

Awake, north wind,
and come, south wind!
Blow on my garden,
that its fragrance may spread everywhere.

SONG OF SOLOMON 4:16

Dwell on the beauty of life. Watch the stars and see yourself running with them.

MARCUS AURELIUS

Dwell on the beauty of life. Watch the stars,
and see yourself running with them.

MARCUS AURELIUS

Be glad... rejoice in the Lord your God, for he has given you the autumn rains because he is faithful.

JOEL 2:23

Be glad . . . rejoice in the L<small>ORD</small> your God, for he has given you the autumn rains because he is faithful.

JOEL 2:23

I like this place
and could willingly
waste my time in it.

WILLIAM SHAKESPEARE

I like this place and could willingly waste my time in it.

WILLIAM SHAKESPEARE

FOR SINCE THE *creation of the world* GOD'S INVISIBLE QUALITIES— HIS ETERNAL POWER AND DIVINE NATURE— HAVE BEEN CLEARLY SEEN.

Romans 1:20

For since the creation of the world God's invisible qualities—his eternal power and divine nature—have been clearly seen, being understood from what has been made, so that people are without excuse.

ROMANS 1:20

NATURE IS THE ART OF GOD

DANTE ALIGHIERI

Nature is the art of God.

DANTE ALIGHIERI

In his hand
are the depths of the earth,
and the mountain peaks
belong to him.

PSALM 95:4

In his hand are the depths of the earth,
and the mountain peaks belong to him.

PSALM 95:4

(GOD) KNEW
EVEN BEFORE HE
CREATED THE WORLD
WHAT BEAUTY HE
WOULD BRING FORTH
FROM OUR LIVES.

Louise B. Wyly

[God] knew even before He created this world what
beauty He would bring forth from our lives.

LOUISE B. WYLY

Satisfy us in the morning with your unfailing love.

PSALM 90:14

Satisfy us in the morning with your unfailing love,
that we may sing for joy and be glad all our days.

PSALM 90:14

The reason birds can fly and we can't is simply because
they have perfect faith, for to have faith is to have wings.

J. M. BARRIE

I lift up my eyes to the mountains—
where does my help come from?
My help comes from the Lord,
the Maker of heaven and earth.

PSALM 121: 1–2

The best remedy
for those who are afraid,
lonely, or unhappy
is to go outside,
somewhere where they can
be quite alone with the
heavens, nature, and God.

ANNE FRANK

The best remedy for those who are afraid, lonely, or
unhappy is to go outside, somewhere where they can
be quite alone with the heavens, nature, and God.

ANNE FRANK

Let all creation rejoice before the Lord.

PSALM 96:13